A PLUME BOOK

I'LL BE DEAD BY THE TIME YOU READ THIS

Shayen Fishman

ROMEO ALAEFF studied biomedical engineering and mathematics at Tulane University before receiving his master of fine arts from the Rhode Island School of Design. His artwork, which includes drawing, photography, film, music, and installations, has exhibited internationally in major museums, galleries, and film festivals. He has been a guest artist and teacher at universities including the Rhode Island School of Design, Brown University, Pratt, and Parsons. Romeo has also been an animation and film editor for many award-winning children's television shows for Nickelodeon, Disney, and PBS.

Sticker versions of some of the animals in this book are featured in the Rizzoli bible of sticker-street art, *Stuck-Up Piece of Crap: Stickers, from Punk Rock to Contemporary Art* alongside works by world-renowned artists such as Andy Warhol, Damien Hirst, Shepard Fairey, and Banksy. The Brooklyn native can be spotted making art in random places like New Orleans, Marfa, Berlin, or Scotland, but he's currently made New York City his home again.

"Every morning, next to my bathroom mirror, Romeo's anxious goldfish reminds me of the fullness of existence; for to be afraid of dying is not to lead a fearful life, but one so precious you don't want to lose it."

—Christian Rattemeyer, associate curator, The Museum of Modern Art

"Romeo's brilliant drawings of cute, contemplative creatures make you laugh, sure, but they also make you think. And they're not just for flipping past; you'll find yourself staring at them —and relating to them—more often than not."

—Isabel Gonzalez, senior editor, *InStyle* magazine

"Romeo's little animals have more tragicomic personality than any character on reality TV, and are certainly more profound!"

—D.B. Burkeman, author of *Stuck-Up Piece of Crap: Stickers, from Punk Rock to Contemporary Art*

I'll Be Dead by the Time You Read This

THE EXISTENTIAL LIFE OF ANIMALS

Romeo Alaeff

A PLUME BOOK

PLUME
Published by Penguin Group

Penguin Group (USA) Inc., 375 Hudson Street, New York, New York 10014, U.S.A. • Penguin Group (Canada), 90 Eglinton Avenue East, Suite 700, Toronto, Ontario, Canada M4P 2Y3 (a division of Pearson Penguin Canada Inc.) • Penguin Books Ltd., 80 Strand, London WC2R 0RL, England • Penguin Ireland, 25 St. Stephen's Green, Dublin 2, Ireland (a division of Penguin Books Ltd.) • Penguin Group (Australia), 250 Camberwell Road, Camberwell, Victoria 3124, Australia (a division of Pearson Australia Group Pty. Ltd.) • Penguin Books India Pvt. Ltd., 11 Community Centre, Panchsheel Park, New Delhi – 110 017, India • Penguin Books (NZ), 67 Apollo Drive, Rosedale, Auckland 0632, New Zealand (a division of Pearson New Zealand Ltd.) • Penguin Books (South Africa) (Pty.) Ltd., 24 Sturdee Avenue, Rosebank, Johannesburg 2196, South Africa

Penguin Books Ltd., Registered Offices: 80 Strand, London WC2R 0RL, England

First published by Plume, a member of Penguin Group (USA) Inc.

First Printing, December 2011
1 3 5 7 9 10 8 6 4 2

Ⓟ REGISTERED TRADEMARK—MARCA REGISTRADA

Alaeff, Romeo.
I'll be dead by the time you read this : the existential life of animals / Romeo Alaeff.
p. cm.
ISBN 978-0-452-29745-6
1. Animals—Humor. 2. Existentialism—Humor. I. Title.
PN6231.A5A44 2011
741.5'6973—dc23
2011026833

Printed in the United States of America

BOOKS ARE AVAILABLE AT QUANTITY DISCOUNTS WHEN USED TO PROMOTE PRODUCTS OR SERVICES. FOR INFORMATION PLEASE WRITE TO PREMIUM MARKETING DIVISION, PENGUIN GROUP (USA) INC., 375 HUDSON STREET, NEW YORK, NEW YORK 10014.

This book is dedicated to my favorite animals:
Ariel, Michaella, and Daniella

Artist's Note

I don't know where the line is drawn between overhearing and eavesdropping. Even if I wanted to, it would be impossible for me to tune out the cell phone conversations, drunken banter at the bar, obliviously loud passengers on an otherwise quiet subway car, elevator whispers, and even the thoughts rattling around in my own head.

About ten years ago, I started writing down little snippets of these conversations in a journal. I'll admit to a bit of selective hearing on my part, but most of what I wrote down was bittersweet, if not downright tragic. It struck me as quintessentially human but also a bit absurd that we regularly torture ourselves with thoughts that seem to be at odds with our very own well-being. After all, if evolution is supposed to improve the species and make it more adaptable, then why aren't we all perpetually happy and well-adjusted?

Animals clearly have a wide range of emotions, but it's sad and sickly funny to imagine them having ones as insane as ours. So in the spirit of milking anthropomorphism, which has served us from before the earliest religions to *Sesame Street*, I started attributing the hundreds of human thoughts I wrote down over the years to these poor animals who don't really deserve to be burdened with our existential angst and neuroses.

Laugh or empathize with "their" pain, but also give thanks. Our animal friends have always graciously been our mirrors, allowing us to truly see, and hopefully laugh at, our tragicomic selves.

—Romeo Alaeff

I've been happier.

I really screwed things up this time.

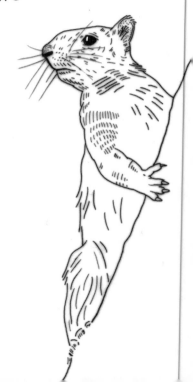

Remember me like I used to be.

Sometimes I feel murderous rage.

Everyone seems so young all of a sudden.

I'm wasting my life.

I enjoy being the victim.

You're going to miss me when I'm gone.

/

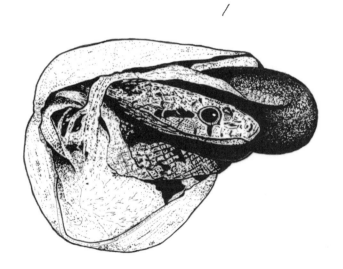

Does that make me crazy?

I have too many secrets.

That'll teach me to follow my instincts.

I'm scared of everything.

 _ I must be in denial.

If I'm asking it must not be love.

I need to live more
in the present.

I live on, false hope.

I think I need therapy.

I need to learn to shut up.

there is so much I wanted to say.

Nobody really knows me.

I drink too much.

Things didn't turn out the way I'd planned.

I'll never be good at anything.

I'm afraid of changing.

I wish I could just start over.

Without you I am nothing.

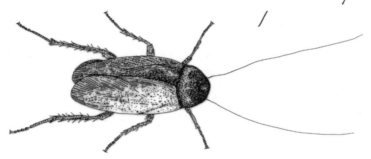

I should have lied.

I have nowhere to run to.

I can't look at you anymore.

I'm afraid of dying.

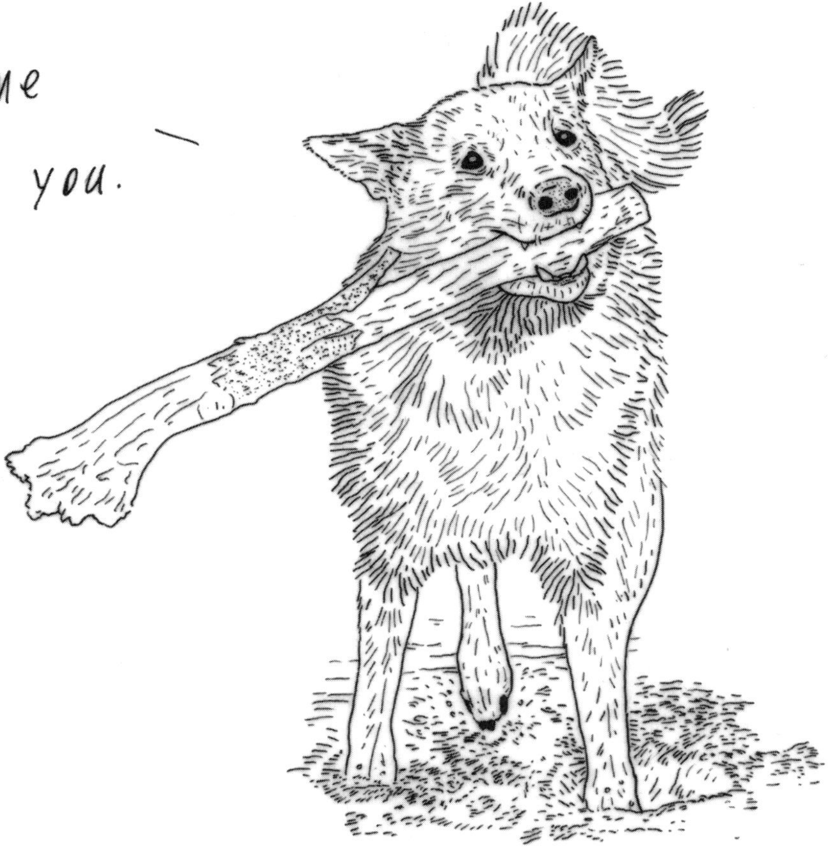
You don't love me
as much as I love you.

I feel ugly today.

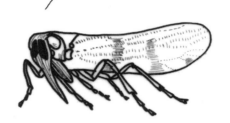

Sometimes I wish I was blind.

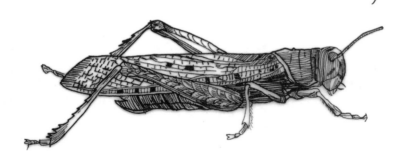

I can fake it a little longer.

I could use a little drama in my life right now.

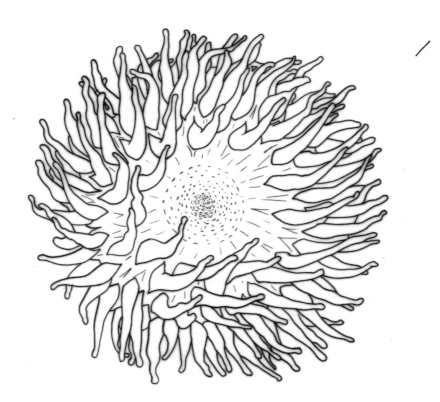

Tell me everything is going to be ok.

I want movie love.

Is this how affairs begin?

I'm going to start making
lists of things —
not to do.

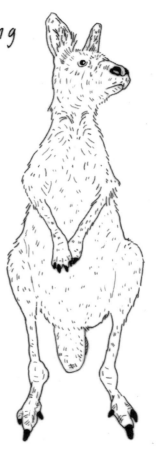

I still think about her.

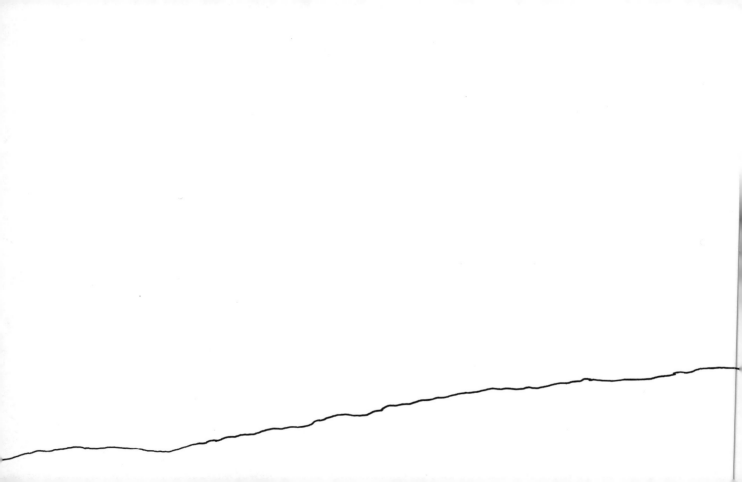

I prefer the misconception you have of me.

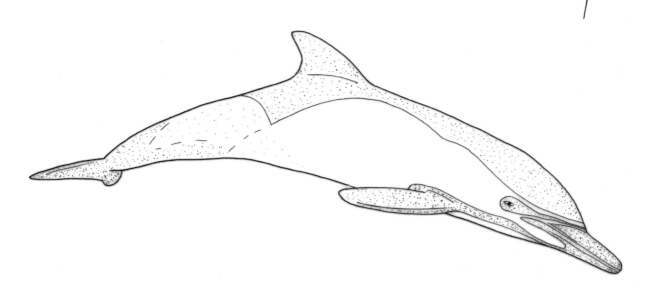

I wish someone would find me.

No one thinks I'm funny.

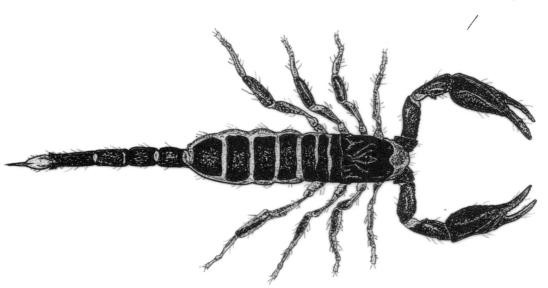

Everyone Sucks.

I can't commit to forever.

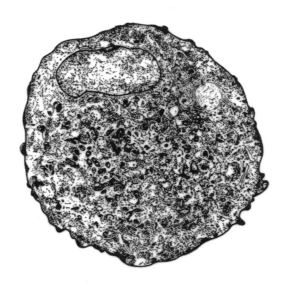

I don't know how to let go.

I don't want to wind up alone.

Nobody loves me.

I can quit anytime.

Things will never be the same.

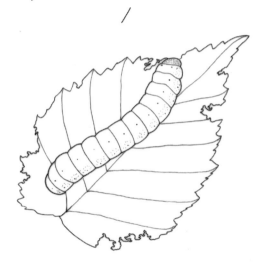

There must be a reason I'm here.

I worried for nothing.

i've really let myself go.

I regret following my heart.

I've lost all my friends.

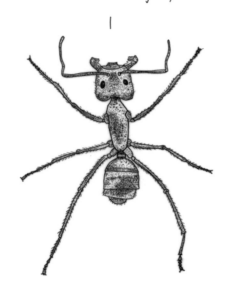

FUCK! —

Life goes on.

I just read your mind.

things got weird.

I'll barely regret this.

I know there's happiness in me somewhere.

Don't pity me.

I need to get out of my own way.

you chose your side, I chose mine.

I guess the honeymoon is over.

I'm damaged goods.

I said I was sorry.

I've lost all sense of purpose.

When am I going to stop breaking hearts?

I've been a jerk.

I wouldn't be good for you.

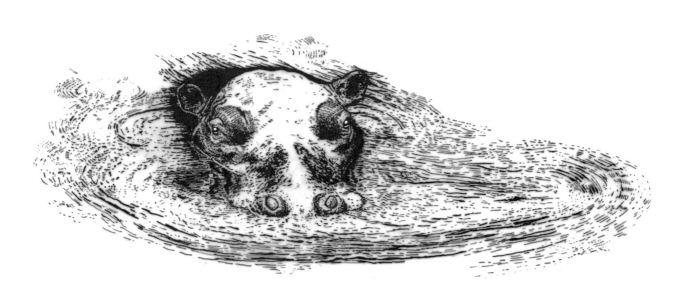

Never forget you're nobody.

I'm living the dream.

The pills aren't working.

you're wrong.

I know I'm going to hell for this.

I'm not dead yet.

I need to cherish this moment.

*   *   *

Acknowledgments

I would like to thank my awesomest agent Alison Schwartz at ICM for believing in me; my übersharp editor Nadia Kashper at Plume for putting up with my craziness and making this book the best it could be; Isabel Gonzalez and Lang Whitaker for making this happen and for cheerleading; and Lisa Dallos at High 10 Media for her cogent insights.

Thank you for their participation to the Wildlife Conservation Society; the American Museum of Natural History, New York; the Smithsonian, DC; the Natural History Museum, London; the Evolution store, New York; and Dover Publications.

Many thanks to the following people for generously letting me use their photos for reference: Julie Larsen Maher, Sam Beattie, Steve and Jackson Neave, Emily Murray, Chen Hui-Chiao, and Christopher Baer.

I would like to thank the collectors who kindly let me steal back my drawings to scan for the book: Moby, Cay Sophie Rabinowitz and Christian Rattemeyer, Meredith Melling Burke, Celerie Kemble, Marisa and Noah Leichtling, Jane Schoenborn, Jenny Galluzzo, Alexis Neophytides, Jenny Salomon, and Alice DuBois.

I would also like to thank the following people who have helped and encouraged me: Allen Houston, who's always got my back, Alex Minott, Alex Navissi, Amy Carickhoff, Anthony Azar, Bemi Aviel and family, Ben Klock, Big-Time Sam, Blaine Palmer, Blair Clarke, the Blum family, Cay Sophie Rabinowitz, Charles Cohen, Chris Baer, Christian Rattemeyer, D. B. Burkeman, Evan Strome, Evelia Godinez, Gabriel Gibson, Jason Ressler, Jessica and Arlo Carroll, Laura Dawn, Lindsay Talley, Lisa Dallos, Meredith Melling Burke, Miranda Gabbard, Moby, Monica LoCascio, Nina Kraviz, Oren Barnoy, Paul Noble and family, Rachel Chatham, Rena Levi, Robin and Andrew Moger and family, Talia Berkowitz, Tania Haddad, and everyone tagging the animal stickers.

Credits

The following drawings were based on photographs by Romeo Alaeff: cover art (fish), pp. 3 (bulldog), 6 (sleeping cat), 10 (staring cat), 25 (butterfly, side view), 36 (sea anemone), 52 (pig with piglets), 83 (fantail fish).

The following drawings were based on photographs by Romeo Alaeff at the Natural History Museum, London: 12 (blowfish), 40 (kangaroo), 62 (dodo), 75 (horse), 76 (crocodile), 78 (warthog). By permission of the Natural History Museum, London.

The following drawings were based on photographs by Romeo Alaeff at the Evolution Store, New York City: 16 (mouse), 20 (ermine), 26 (cockroach), 47 (scorpion), 60 (ant), 69 (crab), 82 (guinea pig). By permission of Alex Minott, the Evolution Store.

The following drawings were based on photographs by Romeo Alaeff at the American Museum of Natural History: 27 (stingray), 45 (dolphin), 53 (anteater), 55 (caterpillar), 73 (shark), 81 (iguana). By permission of the American Museum of Natural History.

The following drawings were based on photographs by Romeo Alaeff at the Central Park Zoo/Wildlife Conservation Society: 32 (monkey), 35 (crowned pigeon), 65 (snow leopard), 70 (snake), 71 (polar bear), 80 (seal). By permission of the Wildlife Conservation Society.

The following drawings were based on photographs by Sam Beattie: pp. 1 (lion), 11 (flying bird), 14 (pygmy elephant), 18 (lioness), 43 (gazelle), 56 (rhino with bird), 58 (rhino), 74 (ox), 77 (hippo). By permission of Sam Beattie.

The following drawing was based on a photograph by Steve Neave: p. 2 (squirrel). By permission of Steve Neave, with thanks to Jackson Neave.

The following drawings were based on etchings and drawings from *Old-Fashioned Animal Cuts*, Dover Publications (1987): pp. 4 (hen), 7 (butterfly), 13 (giraffe), 15 (pig), 21 (moose), 22 (raccoon), 23 (ram), 24 (frog), 28 (hyena), 30 (fantail fish, side view), 33 (locust), 34 (grasshopper), 37 (giant elk), 39 (boar), 46 (unicorn), 48 (rabbit, looking up), 50 (lizard), 54 (bison), 59 (spider), 61 (brachiosaurus), 66 (wasp), 68 (eagle), 72 (turtle). By permission of Dover Publications.

The following drawings were based on photographs by Emily Murray: 5 (grizzly bear), 9 (llama), 17 (meerkat), 31 (dog), 67 (lemur), 79 (red panda). By permission of Emily Murray.

The following drawings were based on photographs of a farm by Christopher Baer: 8 (snake egg), 19 (duck), 38 (fox). By permission of Christopher Baer.

The following drawings were based on photographs at the Smithsonian Museum of Natural History by Christopher Baer: 64 (hamster), 84 (bat). By permission of Christopher Baer and the American Museum of Natural History.

The following drawing was based on a photograph by Julie Larson Maher at the Wildlife Conservation Society: 29 (eagle owl). By permission of Julie Larson Maher and the Wildlife Conservation Society.

The following drawing was based on a photograph by David Hobby: 51 (egg in nest). By permission of David Hobby.

The following drawing was based on a photograph by Chen Hui-Chiao: 57 (sheep). By permission of Chen Hui-Chiao.

The following drawings were based on unknown Web sources: 41 (lovebird), 44 (lovebird), 49 (cell), 63 (house fly).